LESSONS LEARNED FROM MY FRIENDSHIP WITH OCTAVIA E. BUTLER

By

JACQUELINE D. HARRIS

Lesson Learned From My Friendship With Octavia E. Butler

Copyright @2017 Jacqueline D. Harris

ALL RIGHTS RESERVED

No portion of this publication may be reproduced, stored, in any electronic system, or transmitted in any form or by any means, electronic, mechanical, photocopy, recording, or otherwise without written permission from the author. Brief quotations may be used in literary reviews.

ISBN: 978-0-9897678-3-5

FOR PRODUCT AND CONTACT INFORMATION GO TO: **www.sacredtonemasters.com** and

www.amazon.com.

Online ordering is available for all products.

Table of Contents

DEDICATION *5

PREFACE *7

Chapter 1	Octavia Early Years *10	
Chapter 2	How I Met Octavia*18	
Chapter 3	Magic Telephone Call*21	
Chapter 4	First Time Meeting In Person*28	
Chapter 5	Life Lessons From Octavia *37	
Chapter 6	Her Transition *64	
Chapter 7	Closure *79	

About The Author *85

DEDICATION

This book is of course dedicated to my friend and mentor Octavia Estelle Butler. I also want to dedicate it to others in my life that encouraged me to pick up the pen/pencil and write. I've learned so many lessons from you all. I am so thankful our path crossed.

To **Sally Ann Vega**, a Roller Derby skater and star with the Los Angeles Thunderbirds. When I was 9 years old I met you and wanted to be just like you when I grew up. I found out that you wanted to be a writer, a skater and a participate in track and field. So what did I do? I became a writer, a skater and involved in track and field. Thank you for being such a positive influence on my life. I also thank you for reentering my life 4 plus decades later. You were a Godsend.

To **Jane Pauley**, yes that one. When I was about 12 years old, after watching the news, I called NBC in Chicago inquiring about her earrings. Jane took the time to talk to me and invited me to the station. Jane encouraged me to write and allowed me to tag along and watch her work as an anchorwoman at the NBC affiliate in Chicago. That was such a blessing to be able to learn from you. You were always so inspiring and I have never forgotten that. Thank You Jane Pauley.

To **Brenda Griffin**, my 7th grade teacher at Alfred Kohn Elementary School who made me write stories and read them out loud in class. She was one of the most supportive people to ever enter my life.

I thank you all.

PREFACE

I decided to write this book about my friendship with Octavia Butler for several reasons. One, I found while out on book tours after releasing my first book, *Healing And Freedom Through These Sacred Tone Masters*, I found many people after reading about Octavia, asked many questions about her. I found that many people believed so much misinformation about her. I wanted to set the record straight on some of those issues, but I could feel Octavia saying that is not important. For those who did know Octavia, she was an author who many people wanted to know about but did not get the opportunity because Octavia was such a reclusive person.

This book took a while to complete because it was such an emotional and painful story for me to relive and tell. A lot of laughter and tears went into the completion of this book. Octavia was such a special friend to me that her transition left me in such a state of depression. I could not write or do anything that I loved. Thank goodness I was able to force myself to sit and remember. I remembered that there was more laughter to help override the tears.

My second reason for writing this book is the healing achieved from it. It helped me remember the good and joyful times spent with Octavia. It helped me to recall many keys to life that she taught me but I'd forgotten. By trying to not feel the pain of her transition, I found myself putting away the good memories and lessons she shared with me. The completion of this book has helped me remember many life lessons learned from our friendship and her being a Jegna for many others and myself. It also brought back joy to my life because now the wound that surfaced when she transitioned has finally healed.

CHAPTER ONE

Octavia's Early Years

My dear friend Octavia Estelle Butler was born on June 22, 1947 in Pasadena, California, to Octavia Margaret and Laurice James Butler. Octavia was an only child and when she was seven years old, her father died. Her mom and maternal grandmother raised Octavia, whom she loudly declared were some very strict Baptist women. Octavia said she at times felt her mom and grandmother were some fierce mind readers, because they always seem to know what she was doing and they would not allow her to get away with anything. Because Octavia and her mother shared the same name, the family called her mother Octavia and her "Junie" because she was born in the month of June. Octavia use to often joke if she was born in September would the family call her "Septemberie". Octavia would then go through every month of the year giving herself a nickname. Julyee, Octoberie, Novemberie etc. I would roll my eyes to the top of my head so hard I swore I could see the back of my brain. Of course, just as Octavia thought her mom and grandma were reading her mind, I felt she was reading mine and seeing my expressions. Why, because she would say, "stop rolling your eyes at me, Jacqueline. I see you through this phone. Keep it up and I will start calling you Augustie." She would laugh alone. I would say, "The day you start calling me Augustie, is the day I will never answer you."

"Oh you arrogant Leo woman" would be her response.

Octavia's mother was a maid, cleaning up the homes of whites, and would often take her only child to work with her. Octavia would often say she experienced such shame and anger. Shame because of the job her mother did, but extremely angry because of the way she felt her mother was talked down to and treated by the people she worked for. She was also angry, as she would say, at the way her mother just took it and she wanted her to put those people in their place like she did Junie when she spoke out of line. Octavia would often sit under a table in silence reading a book, observing the surroundings or trying to write a story while her mother worked. I remember her saying the one good thing to come out of that job was the family would always give Octavia's mother some amazing books to give to Junie.

Because Octavia was an only child, she found she enjoyed being reclusive. She would often say when she tried to venture out and socialize with people she often found them cruel. Octavia was over 6 feet tall as an adult and she could never remember a time when she was not taller then everybody else around her. She was also dark so she was the victim of cruel name calling by her peers. Octavia said this made her extremely depressed. Octavia found her outlet in writing.

Octavia remember being around 10 or 12 years of age and watching an old science fiction movie called, Devil Girls From Mars. She said it had to be the worst movie she'd ever seen. It sparked Octavia to start to write because she just knew she could write a better movie. Octavia wrote her own sci-fi movie she never published. At the age of 15, Octavia sent her first novel to a publisher. This started her career in receiving rejection letters, as she would state. Octavia felt her job on the planet was to write, so that was all she'd focused on. This was a lesson for be because I've often found it so very challenging to continue doing what it is I'd felt was my purpose when things did not work out.

Octavia would say her teen years were the worst. They were worst then any rejection letter she'd ever gotten from a publishing house or agent. This was a part of her life she would not go much into. But seeing her face and hearing the tones in her voice, you could tell the pain of her experience was still there. She would say the pen and her imagination were the only things keeping her alive. She spent a lot of time crying and writing because she could not understand human cruelty against each other. Octavia said she would just sit in school and daydream. Her lessons were not a priority. The desire to escape this cruel world through her mind and with the pen became an obsession for her. This habitual daydreamer stayed in trouble in school for not doing her work and not participating in class.

Somehow the teachers did not recognize how painfully shy Octavia was. She found one teacher in the 7th grade (Ms. Peters) that recognized Octavia liked to write and permitted her to do that in class. Ms. Peters allowed her to use her creative writing skills and according to Octavia, became like her first editor. Octavia was thrilled to see a story written by her with red marks all over it from Ms. Peters. Octavia said it showed someone cared enough to correct her work. In the ninth grade, Octavia had Ms. Buggs, who happened to be her first African American teacher. Ms. Buggs realized how painfully shy Octavia was and how much standing in front of the classroom hurt her. Ms. Buggs allowed her to present her oral presentations through a recorder or to be typed. That is when Octavia started to excel in school. But as Octavia would say, "I could not stay in ninth grade forever". Octavia loved the 9th grade and was devastated to have to move onto the next grade. Octavia would jokingly say if she were really smart, she would have intentionally failed so that she could repeat the grade again and again to stay with Ms. Buggs. I would sense the pain and would stop or change the conversation because I could tell that Octavia had gone through so much pain and I didn't want to take her down that path again. I also stopped the conversation because it brought a lot of similar painful memories I had as a teen. She was too nice of a person who I loved and wanted nothing but happiness for. So even though I would initiate the conversation about her teen years, I would quickly end it. I just felt it was too much pain she was recalling for both of us.

I could tell writing was the way Octavia handled her

pain and disappointment in humans. Because it was the way I handled my pain. It kept her alive and kept her here long enough to finish the job she would tell you was her destiny. The following quote exemplifies her.

"Although I have worked many jobs to survive, I always knew the only thing I ever wanted to do was write books." *Octavia Estelle Butler*

Octavia would say if she was not a writer, the only job she could see herself working was as a social worker with children. One day we spent hours discussing children on the telephone. She was really fascinated about my job as an investigator of child abuse and neglect. Octavia said she felt so bad for many children because they chose parents that were very irresponsible. She felt children were extremely vulnerable to being abused because of the gullibility of their mothers. I totally agreed with her. You see as a former investigator, I found many mothers responsible for the sexual assault of their children. After all, she is the one who invites the future perpetrator into her home and around her children in her desire to have a man. Many times without knowing his last name. I would talk to Octavia about many of my cases. I remember her saying she didn't think she could emotionally handle that job as an investigator.

I remember during one conversation Octavia said she did not thing there was a young girl who has not been sexually touched by an adult man. I knew the numbers were extremely high but every girl? That floored me because I have always thought this but to hear someone else express it was amazing to me. Now mind you, I knew masses of women who experienced inappropriate touching or a sexual assault that would vehemently argue about the high numbers, as they would disagree with me. Octavia like myself was amazed at the women who would passionately argue as they tried to justify why men sexually assaulted women and children.

This conversation inspired me to write a book. You see I have worked as an investigator of abuse and neglect of children for almost 20 years. So I had a lot of stories to tell. Of course that book has been delayed due to so many of life distractions Thanks to my remembering some of life lessons learned from Octavia, I can now side step and handle those obstacles and get busy on that book.

CHAPTER 2

HOW I MET OCTAVIA ESTELLE BUTLER

After I read *Parable of the Sower* in 1996, there was no doubt in my mind that Octavia Butler's talent as a novelist was unsurpassed. The book written in 1993, set in futuristic Los Angeles, predicts the demise of civil society -- government gone amuck, global warming, high unemployment, and barbaric behavior. In many ways, I found the book to be prophetic. The way things are going today, many others are coming to the same conclusion about the book. This book is really selling, studied and talked about on social media because of the atmosphere in the world today. It truly is a book of prophecy. Parable Of The Sower is bringing a brand new audience to Octavia. I hear movies are going to be done on a few of her books. This is great but I sure wish Octavia had gotten that audience when she was alive.

I didn't start out as a science fiction buff; I preferred reading science textbooks or encyclopedias, sports magazines, cultural and history books – anything that I could get my hands on – but definitely not science fiction. I was one of those people who thought that the genre of science fiction consisted only of Star Trek and Star Wars. That is, until a friend gave me a copy of Parable Of The Sower (Which falls under the genre of science fiction), after reading this wonderful gem, I was hooked. I right away went out and purchased the two books, Mind of My Mind and Wild Seed.

I was in a reading group and I recommended Parable Of The Sower to them. We all read the book and got together to discuss it. All of us were immediately in love with the writings of Octavia Butler and thought she was a genius before the McArthur Foundation did. We just didn't have a quarter of a million dollars to give her as they did. In fact, we read the book several times. The next thing I knew I was trying to buy every book she ever wrote. I was just into her writings and I just felt we were from the same line of women.

One night in 1999 after reading her book, *Mind of My*

Mind for the umpteenth time, I decided to write her. Since I had read practically everything she had ever written, I felt as if I'd known her my entire life. I wanted to tell her how much I admired her work.

Chapter Three

The Magic Telephone Call

It was no secret Octavia Butler was a brilliant writer, a shining star in the science fiction universe, but she was also a self-described recluse – and one who fiercely guarded her privacy. Therefore, I decided to contact her through her publisher in hopes they would forward my letter to her. Maybe one day I would receive a handwritten thank you note. Was I surprised at what I did receive? So I wrote her a letter, sealed it in an envelope and put a stamp on it. All that was missing was an address for Octavia.

I went to the library and got online and started my search. Tons of information was available about her books but nothing about how to contact her. All of a sudden, a telephone number popped up, I decided to take a chance and call it. A woman answered the phone, and I explained that because Octavia Butler was one of my favorite authors, I had written her a letter and needed an address to mail it to her. The woman was not forthcoming. She asked how I had obtained the telephone number. I explained to her the number popped up when I typed Octavia Butler's name in a search engine on the Internet. I don't think she believed me, so we went back and forth for about fifteen minutes.

"Impossible, this number is not on the Internet," the woman vehemently insisted. It never occurred to me a publishing house would not list their number online.

Finally, I said in my *I have had enough of this* tone, "Can you please just give me an address, a P.O. Box number, or anything so I can mail this letter to this woman?"

"Why do you want to write to Octavia?" she asked.

I exhaled the breath of frustration. I mean does every publishing house put you through the third degree in order to write to one of their authors? Without thinking, these words fell out of my mouth. "I feel as if I know Octavia Butler, and I absolutely adore her writing. I was finally able to find myself in her words."

And there was silence in the earth because I felt I revealed a little too much about me to this stranger and I was trying to figure out how to take those words back. That made me extremely uncomfortable. The lady broke the silence by saying,

"Jacqueline…that is your name, right?"

"Yes," I replied.

"That is good to hear. This is Octavia Butler, and you have somehow called my home," she said.

"Yeah, right," I replied sarcastically.

Since I am the ultimate cynic, I summarily dismissed her remarks and continued to ask for an address to write to the author.

For the next thirty to forty-five minutes, the woman tried to convince me that she was in fact Octavia Butler. So, I decided to quiz this imposter about Octavia Butler books and her characters. Although, she never hesitated and answered every question correctly, I still didn't believe her.

"Why don't you believe me?" Octavia asked.

I shrugged my shoulders as if she could see them through the telephone.

Silence in the earth again.

I didn't believe her until we started to talk about Mitochondrial DNA. I stated that Mitochondrial DNA was passed only from mother to daughter. This woman told me that was not true. So, I was really sick of this conversation.

I mean really? First, she was giving me a hard time about getting an address. Then, she claimed to be Octavia, and now, she was correcting me? That was a bit much for this woman (me) born under the astrological sign of Leo to take.

However, this woman stated that the Mitochondrial DNA is passed from the mother to her sons and daughters, but the daughters can only pass it to her children. She explained it in a way that made sense to me. **That's when** something clicked in my heart and told me this woman was, in fact, Octavia Estelle Butler.

I was so embarrassed that I immediately regressed to that of a two-year-old child. I stuttered and stumbled my way through sentences. I was nervous and sweating. I felt as if I had somehow invaded a sacred space. All I wanted to do was hang up the telephone and crawl into a corner.

All of a sudden, I heard snickering and then loud laughter. Was she now really laughing at me?
This somehow proved to be so hilarious for Octavia and she could not stop laughing. While laughing, Octavia asked

me why I made her take all of that time to convince me that she was who she said she was?

"Life is not that easy for me," I responded.

Octavia said, "It was this time, you found my unlisted home telephone number on the computer. You were lucky in that I answered the telephone when it was an unknown number to me. This is something I never do. You were lucky that I didn't hang up the telephone immediately. Now that is something I have been known to do." My response was, "Damn, I am lucky."

We both laughed and ended up talking for more than five hours that evening. We chatted as if we were old friends, the best of friends. At the end of the conversation, I asked Octavia once again to give me an address so I could stay in touch with her.

She burst out in laughter again and said, "Jacqueline, you are welcome to call me here at my home whenever you want to".

And I did.

I said, "What about this letter I wrote you? I spent a lot of time on this letter." Octavia said, "OMG you are so stubborn and persistent, mail the damn letter to this address." She sounded frustrated as she gave me her address. This time I burst out in laughter.

As time went on, I would call Octavia and she would call me. When my telephone would ring and I saw a 206 area code, I wanted to answer the telephone on the 1/100th of the first sound of the ring, but I played it cool. I let it ring a couple of times before I answered. I had a feeling Octavia knew what I was doing. Why do I say that? Well, sometimes when I answered the phone she would be laughing. I believed she was psychic, just like she believed her mother and grandmother were. Though I felt this about Octavia, I still tried to hide things from her.

Octavia and I would talk on the telephone about everything from movies to politics. We discussed literature, and sometimes we would talk about sports, a topic she had very little interest in but she participated in because she knew that it was something I loved. It hit me one day when she started talking about the magnificent centerfielders who played for the amazing Oakland Raiders. This was the end of our sports talk.

CHAPTER 4
MEETING FOR 1ST TIME IN PERSON

During the spring of 2000, she invited me to join her in Baltimore, Maryland. She was being honored at the Baltimore Sci-Fi Convention. I didn't give it a second thought. I jumped at the opportunity, and then I jumped in my car and made the thirteen-hour trip from Milledgeville, Georgia to Baltimore, Maryland. The two of us toured Charm City that weekend. Octavia showed me all of the places she had visited more than thirty-six years ago while conducting research for her book *Kindred*.

We walked to the old Greyhound bus station on Fayette Street. I couldn't believe she traveled on Greyhound. She actually "rode the dog" all the way from California to Baltimore, Maryland to do research for the book Kindred, because she was afraid to fly at the time. Imagine, three days on Greyhound and Octavia was well over six feet tall. Octavia came to Maryland to do research at a plantation in Eastern Shore, Maryland. At the time, she had to walk close to five miles to catch a bus to Eastern Shore. Octavia also spent a lot of time at the Enoch Pratt Library, the Maryland Historical Society and she also traveled to Mount Vernon, Virginia to do research at George Washington's plantation. Octavia endured many trials to accomplish the mission she was specifically put on this planet to carry out – she stayed the course. I still cannot believe she traveled on the bus from California to Maryland. Three days aboard a Greyhound bus amazed me. Why? Well, on occasion, I will travel from Maryland to New York by bus. The trip is only four-five hours, but you'd think I was on the bus for 127 hours the way I carried on. I am so antsy. Therefore, it amazes me that Octavia had the ability to spend three days on a bus traveling across the United States. Growing up, I remember riding the bus from Chicago to Memphis. I personally think the bus seats have gotten smaller as I've gotten older. I swear I had more space on the buses when I was younger. I'd often imagine what did she write on those long trips.

We walked over to Travelers' Aid – a place she had gone for information on where to find lodging during her stay. Travelers' Aid was directly across the street from the Greyhound Bus Station and they had given her coupons to eat at the Lexington Market. They had also found her a place to stay while she was in Baltimore. We then headed over to Lexington Market on West Lexington Street, between Eutaw and Greene Streets in the heart of downtown Baltimore, which was one of her favorite places for her daily meals. Octavia loved to sit and watch the many characters walking up and down the street. Octavia said, "you know Jacqueline, you could have furnished your entire house from the street vendors in the area. I laughed and told her about being able to do the same thing on a train ride in Chicago. As we strolled down the street toward the historic Lexington Market, I wanted everyone we passed to know I was with Octavia Butler – the first science-fiction writer to receive the prestigious MacArthur "Genius" Award.

And a multi award-winning novelist.

And one of the nicest people I have ever met.

And my friend.

Oh and as we exited the market, a truck rolled by with a guy yelling that he was selling bed frames and mattresses. Octavia looked at me and said, " It seems some things have remained the same."

During our walking tour, we found a quaint little place called Shane's Sandwich Shops on W. Fayette Street. We placed our orders and then talked for hours about everything under the sun. I tried to keep up, but I was no match for her. Octavia possessed an encyclopedic mind. She loved science and was sadden the most by humans and their behavior towards each other. She didn't hold out much hope for the human race. Humans to her seem to strive on hierarchy, racism, sexism, and every other kind of ism. She felt that it was very sad that the only time humans came together on a grand scale was when they felt they had a common enemy or some major disaster has occurred. In multiple interviews and essays, Butler explained her view of humanity as inherently flawed by an innate tendency towards hierarchical thinking which leads to intolerance, violence and, if not checked, the ultimate destruction of our species. I said I felt that humans were like food that has been taken out of the oven too soon. She loved that.

I figured that I would brush up on the topics that we enjoyed talking about. Science and writing were two topics that Octavia enjoyed. However, something happened that showed me that I was going to have a problem with this friendship. The problem was the topic of food. At the time I was a vegetarian and she was vegan. I made the mistake of ordering a veggie sub with cheese in her presence. She instantly started fussing at me. She was not going to let me eat in peace with a vegetarian sub with cheese on it. I told her that I would have to work my way to becoming a vegan. Octavia politely said, "Jacqueline that is a bunch of bullshit." I instantly said to myself, "Note to self, do not eat with this woman again."

Now a little information about the book Kindred, that had Octavia travel across the country on a Greyhound bus. For those who are not familiar with Kindred, it is a book written by Octavia in 1976. The book is about Dana, a 26-year-old modern black woman who is, celebrating her birthday with her new husband when she is snatched abruptly from her home in California and transported to an antebellum south plantation. Rufus, the white son of the plantation owner, is drowning, and Dana has been summoned to save him. Dana is drawn back repeatedly through time to the slave quarters, and each time the stay grows longer, more difficult, and more dangerous until it is uncertain whether or not Dana's life will end, long before it has a chance to begin.

I asked Octavia what made her decide to write a book like *Kindred*. Octavia said she wrote Kindred to deal with the shame and anger she felt towards her mother who was a servant in the home of whites. Octavia's mother would take her to work with her and Octavia recalls her mother being treated badly. Octavia would say that she stayed angry with her mother for not standing up for herself. Octavia felt her mother should have stood up for herself more. Octavia said, as she got older she realized her mother endured the cruel treatment to make a better life for her. Octavia also talked about conversations she had with so-called black power/conscious men who ignorantly said people like her mother were traitors and should have been killed. That angered her because she knew how hard her mother worked and the sacrifices she made to put a roof over her head and food on the table for them. Octavia said,

"It is so easy for people to say what they would do in certain situations, until they are placed in them.

"And that my friend was the basis for me to write the book *Kindred*".

According to Octavia, it took her getting older to realize what was going on. When I was asked what did she mean by what was going on, Octavia would say, the wicked hierarchical sexist, racist, and colorist systems humans have set up, accepted and see no reason to change on this planet.

<u>"Simple peck-order bullying", she wrote in her essay "A World without Racism", "is only the beginning of the kind of hierarchical behavior that can lead to racism, sexism, ethnocentrism, classism, and all the other 'isms' that cause so much suffering in the world."</u>

Octavia also said that as she was growing up, she never saw a heroine that looked like her so she set out to place them in her books for others like her. She truly believed that if you didn't see yourself in something, writing afforded you the opportunity to change that. Octavia didn't believe in waiting for others to do something, especially if you had the capability to do it yourself. Octavia had no idea the effect her books have had on my life until I told her. I raise my head a little higher because of Octavia and her books. I would tell Octavia seeing a black heroine was something that I didn't have growing up and how much it meant to me to see them. She would often blush when I would tell her that she was my black heroine. The Baltimore trip sealed our friendship forever.

Octavia officially became my Jegna.

Jegna is an Ethiopian (Amharic) word that means someone who has been tested in struggle or battle. A Jegna is someone who has shown determination and courage in protecting the culture. Someone who teaches and nurtures, and helps develop others by advancing the culture. A Jegna also is one who has produced an exceptionally high quality of work.

I loved questioning and talking to Octavia. She said sometimes she felt as if she was in an interrogation room when we would talk. I would stop but she would say, please continue. Octavia said one of her favorite plays was a sci-fi play called Ruby, The Adventures of a Galactic Gumshoe. She said I reminded her of Ruby with my questions, sense of humor, sarcasm and cynicism. I thought that was hilarious because for many years I'd worked as an investigator. I said that I'd never heard of the play. Octavia said she would make it a priority to send me the play, after questioning whether I lived under a rock because I hadn't heard of the play. She was always a woman of her word and sent me a box filled with cassette tapes of the play. Octavia wanted to make sure that I listen to the play. To this day I absolutely love the play. I've listened so many times.

CHAPTER 5
<u>LESSONED LEARNED</u>

During a conversation with Octavia, I informed her I was about to move closer to the Atlanta area and how stressed out I was about the move. I was talking about the stress of packing about 5 containers of books. Octavia told me when she moved from California to Seattle, she had more than three hundred boxes of books to transport and had hired an eighteen-wheeler to ensure that her books arrived safely. All I could do was say are you kidding me as I visualized an 18-wheeler full of books. I scratched my head and relaxed as my stress dissipated immediately. In fact, I remembered when Octavia was moving from California to the State of Washington. I became frightened for her. Why? Because I had heard that a lot of racist lived in that state. Silly me, like they didn't live in every state. Octavia said she couldn't think of a place where racists don't live on this planet. Besides, they are a bunch of cowards who get off on the energy of fear they get from you. Octavia said she'd lived a life of fear until her late 20's. That was such a burden to carry. She said at this point in her life she refused to entertain fear. Octavia would chuckle and say, how could you question me moving from California to Seattle Washington and you just moved from Chicago to probably the smallest town in Georgia and not even Atlanta. That helped me to see how courageous I was.

"First forget inspiration. Habit is more dependable. Habit will sustain you whether you're inspired or not. Habit will help you finish and polish your stories. Inspiration won't. Habit is persistence in practice."

Octavia use to love to call me and ask me what was I working on. I remember for a couple of weeks I told her nothing. I said that every day I would sit down to write and nothing would come out. I had a bad case of writer's block. I told Octavia that I was not inspired to write, so I would write when I get inspired again. Octavia said waiting on inspiration is bullshit. I was stunned because that is how I would always write, when I was inspired.

One of the many lessons I was blessed to learn from Octavia was how to cure writer's block. Octavia helped me cure writer's block from that point on when she said, "I remember you telling me how much you love that horrible combination of sunflower seeds and ginger-ale. I don't know who in their right mind would eat that combination but you do and you eat that combination all the fucking time. So this is obviously you and it is what you do. Take that mess and go to the park and just sit there and watch the people, the birds, the grass grow, the clouds move, your eyelashes grow. (Remember I told you Octavia had a major sense of humor) Octavia said after you have completed your jaunt in the park, come home and just write what you saw that day. But always remember this, writing when inspired is for the birds. Writing should be a habit more

39

then an inspiration. Writing should be something you do EVERYDAY. You must make writing a habit and not something by inspiration.

Inspiration is short-lived. What if you only get inspired three times a year? You mean to tell me that you are only going to write three times a year? If you do that you are in trouble. A lot of people find themselves writing due to inspiration. You must always find out what words mean and when you look up the word inspiration, you will find it means fleeting. What you need to do is write something everyday. Even if what you write has nothing to do with the topic you want to publish. What you will find is that you may start off writing about another topic, but eventually you will find yourself writing a word, grasp an idea or have a thought that would lead you right back to your topic to publish. Always work on making writing everyday a habit and I guarantee you will find yourself finishing your project."

Another lesson learned from Octavia was to always carry business cards with me. Over the years, she would ask whether or not I had taken her advice.

"So, Jacqueline, did you have your cards made up yet?"

"Not yet, Ms. Butler, I'll get them later." That was my standard response to Octavia's inquiries.

In fact, I still have the business card she gave to me in the year 2000. I bring all this up to show some of the many ways Octavia provided tips to me on writing and life. Whenever Octavia would tell me that she was conducting research for a new book, I would make it my business to locate materials to send to her that might be of some assistance. Octavia mentioned that she was looking for information on the Black Native Americans. I went out and searched and found the book Black Indians by William Katz. I mailed the book to her and felt so proud and happy. Those were good times. They were not always good.

Sometimes, Octavia would call and ask me to read to her some of my work. Of course, I would instantly become unable to read or speak. I was still intimidated by her reputation. I was also extremely insecure when it came to my writing. I mean this was Octavia Butler who the McArthur Foundation said was a genius and gave a quarter of a million dollars too. At the time I was not sure if I would recover if she said, "Oh Jacqueline, your writing sucks." I couldn't imagine coming back from something like that happening. I had always placed Octavia on a pedestal, and it became apparently clear later on that she was not having or liking it.

If I had a problem, Octavia would sense it, even though I tried to pretend that my life was great. I laugh now at my futile attempts to mask what was going on in my life from her. I remember in August of 2000, I broke two of my toes when I tripped over some dumb bells in the floor of my house. Dumbbells that I passed so many times and said I would move them later. I woke up one morning and tripped over them while walking to the kitchen in bare feet. I heard the crack but never thought they were broke. I actually put on shoes and went to work. While at work the pain became unbearable and I had to go to the emergency room. After returning from the hospital, I was so angry with the doctor who would not give me a pair of crutches. Doctor William Thompson said that I needed to take that time and sit down and think about some things. Doctor Thompson said, "I am not going to give you crutches because you would be all over the place with them and your toes could heal quicker if you would stay off your feet for a few weeks". After getting home, Octavia called and said, "Jacqueline, I was thinking about you and wanted to make sure you were ok." I told her what happened with the weights and 2 broken toes and how my doctor took it upon himself to deny me a pair of crutches. I was angry and venting. Octavia felt Dr. William Thompson was one of the smartest doctors on the planet, because he found a way to force me to sit still and write. I must thank Dr. Thompson because I finally put in motion my first book, *'Healing and Freedom Through These Sacred Tone Masters'*.

Octavia would tell me to focus on the writing and she would walk me through the world of publishing. So that is exactly what I did. I focused on my writing. I never ever thought I would not get the chance to learn about the world of publishing from Octavia.

Octavia would call and ask me to read my works to her. Octavia would on so many occasions also call to remind me that associates were one thing and friends were another and that I needed to make sure I could distinguish the difference.

"Jacqueline, my friends call me Octavia and you are one of my dear friends." One of the main things Octavia said to me was, "Jacqueline, because you are a sensitive person, you really need to know the difference between sympathy and empathy. If you don't you will stay stuck and an emotional wreck." It took many years before I got the lesson in that statement. The sad part is because I'd forgotten this lesson and the difference; I went through one of the worst times in my life. Only to find out that if I would have not blocked out so much of remembrances of Octavia, I would have alleviated so much heartache in my life.

I've learned so many lessons from Octavia, but <u>Patience</u> is the virtue she instilled in my heart. I am not always the most patient one. It is a lesson I have been striving to master for as long as I can remember. I always felt that I never asked for much, which in itself is not a good thing. But, I felt the things that I did ask for should have been given to me as soon as I asked for them. I wanted what I wanted, and I wanted it when I asked for it. Today, I can see the internal temper tantrums I would throw if denied my request. Although I was not patient, I somehow expected…no, I demanded that people practice patience with me at all times.

When I would encounter a situation where someone had committed a wrongdoing to me, I was quick to dismiss him or her from my life. I had no patience for others' shortcomings. But, I had the audacity to not be able to deal with someone dismissing me from his or her lives. I learned later that sometimes it is okay to dismiss people from your life. I just needed to be balanced and not freak out if it happens to me.

I now know that I exhibited the shortest amount of patience when dealing with myself. I also now know that I was living the life of a hypocrite. That was then. Now, I am extremely patient with myself, which makes for a very patient being when dealing with others. Another major lesson learned from Octavia.

As my friendship with Octavia blossomed, I became aware that her life was showing me what it means to be patient and have patience when dealing with others and myself.

Octavia helped me face my fears by sharing how she overcame some of hers. Octavia telephoned me one day and was inquiring about my fears. Now mind you I was sitting and stressing over a fear at the time. I let her know whatever fears I wanted to share at the time; I would be a fool to share them with her. You see Octavia was the type of person who would always laugh at the things she was not supposed to laugh at. You know those things your mother went upside your head for laughing at? I was convinced she would laugh at me so I was not going to give her laughter for the day at my expense. Octavia would snicker and say, "Jacqueline, you must not know how persistent I am, because if you did you would know one way or another I will get it out of you. Now I really want to know." Octavia then said, "Since you want to keep secrets from me, can you at least tell me how do you handle your fears? I thought I was being really clever by saying that I don't bother with them. As long as I leave them alone, they will leave me along. Whew, was I being arrogant with my ignorance. Of course I learned later in life that my ignoring and running away from my fears was not the best thing for me. Your fears always will find a way of tapping you on your shoulders to let you know they are still around.

Octavia said, "Even though you won't share any of your fears with me, I will share one with you. Octavia decided to work on a fear that had paralyzed her since she was a child. Octavia said she use to find herself going so far out of her way to avoid these things. She said she would walk 3-5 blocks out of her way when she saw a group of birds. Octavia use to love to go and sit in the park but that fucking Alfred Hitchcock movie screwed it up for her. Her words not mine. The movie The Birds totally traumatized Octavia. She said, "if I am enjoying myself in the park and see a few birds looking at me, I will get up and go home, quickly. You know how nature likes to play with you sometimes? Well, one time, as I was leaving the park, the birds just followed me. I just knew they were going to be the death of me."

Octavia said she was not clear what brought this on, but she had decided to overcome her fear of birds.

"How are you going to do that Octavia?"

"I'll keep you posted."

So as time went on, Octavia would call and tell me her journey to overcoming her fear of birds. Do you want to know what she did? It truly amazed me. Octavia said she would go to the park and sit and watch people feed the birds. She sat down one day and a bird was looking at her. She decided to allow the bird to come close to her. She said she was shaking and sweating profusely but she eventually found herself chatting with the bird. Octavia said that she told the birds her fears of them, how Alfred Hitchcock ruined the relationship for a lot of people with birds. How she no longer wanted to fear them. Octavia said she was stammering and stuttering because she was so scared. She also said she know people were passing by her and probably saying, look at this crazy tall black woman talking to this bird. Octavia said she told the bird she would come to the park every other day to talk to them. Octavia said the birds lessened her anxiety. The birds would come and stand by her for long periods of time. The birds would not get to close to make her nervous. The birds would sit in front of her as if they were in school listening to her. Octavia said she told the birds that she was so afraid of them and how she wanted to eliminate that fear. Octavia started putting food at a distance from her for the birds to eat. The birds would go and eat the food and come and sit right back in front of her. She got enough courage to feed the birds herself while she was sitting. Octavia said when the birds approached her she realized she didn't die. She then decided to have the bird first sit on her leg. In the end, Octavia said she stood one day and allowed the birds to cover her arms, shoulders and legs. When she opened her eyes and saw that she was still on the planet earth and not dead, she knew she'd conquered that fear. So now Octavia does not walk blocks out of her way to avoid a bunch of birds. She walks right beside them because as she said, "It is so rude to walk in the middle of a group".

Octavia said that I was doing a horrible disservice to myself by ignoring my fears. They are like spoiled children, who become louder and louder the more you ignore them. I knew she was right. Because of that lesson, I have worked on conquering a lot of my fears. I was always afraid of heights and getting on boats. One year, I remembered her story and decided, if Octavia could conquer her bird fear, surely I could conquer my height and boat fears. I took a trip to Toronto, Canada to visit the museums and while there; I decided to go to the top of the CN Building, which at the time was the second tallest building in the world. I too, noticed that I didn't die. I was drenched from nervous sweating but I was still alive. I got bold and brought a ticket for a boat ride around Lake Superior. I was nausea but I found that I actually enjoyed the trip and didn't drown from this imaginary capsizing of the boat that always frightened me.

I'd forgotten all of these great lessons taught to me by Octavia because it was so painful dealing with her transition. Because of that, I found myself falling right back into the hole of evading my fears and yes letting them get the best of me. Once I started writing this book, I also found myself climbing out of the hole of fear and facing them more.

Octavia continued to write despite tons of rejection letters. She conquered dyslexia, extreme shyness, and an obsession with daydreaming. Today, she is considered one of the greatest writers ever -- a testament to her courage, determination, and patience.

What pulled me toward Octavia was her writing on the back of many of her books. As I wrote earlier in this book, I found myself through Octavia and her writing. This is how she described herself and it is so me.

"I am comfortably asocial—a hermit in the middle of Seattle—a pessimist if I am not careful, a feminist, a Black, a former Baptist, an oil and water combination of ambition, laziness, insecurity, certainty, and drive."

Take out the Seattle part and she just described me.

Photo Taken in Baltimore, Maryland with Octavia

The picture above was taken in Baltimore, Maryland at the Balticon Convention. I loved teasing Octavia about her wearing and setting off people with attention deficit disorder shirt. She would laugh so hard and respond with words I can't begin to tell because children may be reading. Every time I see this picture I smile. It was our first time meeting and such a great moment. I was so happy this day even with the worst haircut of my life.

Here are thirteen of the magnificent works and keys to life that Octavia Estelle Butler left for the world:

1) Patternmaster (1976)
2) Mind of My Mind (1977)
3) Survivor (1978)
4) Kindred (1979)
5) Wild Seed (1980)
6) Clay's Ark (1984)
7) Dawn (1987)
8) Adulthood Rites (1988)
9) Imago (1989)
10) Parable of the Sower (1993)
11) Bloodchild and Other Stories (1995)
12) Parable of the Talents (1998)
13) Fledgling (2005)

I would also like to share another lesson learned from Octavia. She would not allow any circumstance that occurred in her life to physically stop her from achieving her goals. I, on the other hand did not always establish that pattern. Many times I found myself blaming my circumstances and life for me would come to a complete stop. I would truly become immobile. Octavia said certain situations made her stronger and everything went into a story for her. I was so happy to hear and remember this and could relate too it because that was so much like my early awkward teen years, and throughout my life I would go through this. I was teased, very sensitive, and painfully shy and could only really relate to a pen and paper. I too had a teachers, a news anchor, a roller derby star, a medical doctors and others who entered my life and encouraged my writings. They are listed in the dedication section of this book. They all supported me and forced me out of my shell.

I was one whom had forgotten many times their purpose on this planet. I would often find myself trying to invent another purpose for my life. But, I would always find myself guided back to writing. Many times I have found that it was Octavia who would always guide me back to writing by doing this simple thing. Octavia would accomplish this goal by calling my house and asking me to read to her what I'd written that week. Lord knows many weeks I did not write anything and knew I needed to have something new for her. I could hear the disappointment in her voice. That kept me on top of my game. I never wanted to disappointment her. I must say that I found myself going extreme lengths of time not writing anything and finding that Octavia is no longer here in the physical to help me get back on point. Now I have to do it myself and I find it very hard to do.

Another lesson learned after a conversation with Octavia. She asked me what genre did I think I would write in. My response was the usual, "I don't know". At the time I was truly anti sci-fi. In my mind, I, like many others thought sci-fi was Star Wars and Star Trek. I have no disrespect for those who love those shows but I did not watch them. I would tell Octavia that I didn't consider her sci-fi and that is why I could read her books. I never considered Octavia a sci-fi writer and she herself felt she crossed many genres. She reminded me of the great vocalist and entertainer Nancy Wilson. Nancy never wanted to be pigeon –holed into being classified as just a jazz singer. She felt she was soul, r & b, rock, and jazz, actress, radio host, interviewer and a singer/songwriter who crossed all genres. That is how Octavia felt about her writings. When I told her about some of my unreleased material, Octavia would chuckle and say, "Oh, Jacqueline the way you write, the discussions we have, trust me they will more then likely call you a sci-fi writer." That broke my heart because at the time, all I knew about science fiction was Star Wars and Star Trek. I rebelled internally against that statement but later told myself that if Octavia is considered the greatest in that genre…it could not be that bad. At the time, I had no idea of other science fiction writers of color. Some years later, Octavia told me about Steven Barnes and Tananarive Due and how I needed to learn more about the genre before I condemn them all to hell. We laughed. I have not released the books of mine that Octavia considered Sci-Fi but they are coming soon.

    I remember saying that I could not see the correlation between me writing a book about women using their extra sensory abilities of telepathy, intuition, psychometry and clairvoyance and science fiction. I would argue that is not science fiction. Many women use one, two or maybe three, hell, you even use them when you call me and say, "Jacqueline, I felt something troubling you and am calling to check on you." Is that not intuition?

"No one is saying you are wrong but dear that would be labeled science fiction, whether you like it or not. There are some things that some people can do that others can't or are afraid to. To the ones who can't, they label it as something phenomenal or outer worldly. Remember the witch-burning era? Some women were during natural things of nature but to the ones who could not do those things, it was either outer worldly, or the devil. Jacqueline stop fighting and come on over to the world of science fiction or the dark side." Then she would do her James Earl Jones, Darth Vader laugh. I would just shake my head as if to say, "what is wrong with this woman".

Of course, Octavia would break out in laughter saying, "I can visualize the disdain on your face." Because I did not find this at all funny, this made her laugh even more. Octavia was definitely the person who knew how to make herself laugh, which I admired; I just didn't like the fact that many times it was at my expense. Octavia was definitely a woman who could find humor anywhere. I always said that Octavia was the type of person who laughed at the things we were taught not to laugh at as children. This grew me closer to her because I shared in that same ability except when it was at my expense.

This was another thing I wanted to share with people about Octavia. When I would give speeches about my first book, *"Healing and Freedom Through These Sacred Tone Masters",* of which a chapter is in it about Octavia, so many people would ask certain questions about her. So many people thought she was this morbid, brooding, always serious, humorless person all the time. Please don't get me wrong, there were times she could be, but for the most part, she had a huge sense of humor. Most people did not know this about her. Octavia loved to laugh and we spent hours talking and laughing about everything. I think most may have thought of her as I did when I first met her. I thought she was this humorless, unapproachable woman who sat on a pedestal because of her works. I am so glad to have been blessed to have the opportunity to really get to know her and be considered one of her friends.

I noticed that Octavia became tired of me approaching her with a look of awe on my face. She kept telling me to stop it and treat her as a friend and not whoever the hell I was thinking she was in my brain. I tried but kept falling short. So I later learned that Octavia created a situation that caused me to take/snatch/pull her off the pedestal and changed our friendship forever and for the better. Octavia said she'd figured out how my ego works and what were my trigger words and how to use them. She said she'd figure out how to be removed off the pedestal I had placed her on. That is exactly what happened. We loved to talk about science; once I started engaging in the conversation, Octavia all of a sudden started hurling obscenities and insults at me.

"Jacqueline, that is fucking crazy."

"Jacqueline are you sure you went to school because that was retarded."

I got quiet like my mother does right before she is about to let you have it. I was seething and all of a sudden these words fell out of my mouth. "Listen, I don't care how many books you wrote, who said you are a genius, or how many awards you may have won, but you don't ever talk to me that way ever again. To make my point, I had the nerve to say, are we clear?" I was rocking my knee because I had reached the highest level of pissitivity (If it is not a word, it is now). Instead of responding with I'm sorry, my bad, or any other type of an apology, which I was waiting for, Octavia, lets out a loud laughter and drops the telephone.

Imagine this, I am sitting there boiling on my end and she is cracking up on the other end. She finally picks back up the phone and says, "I bet I'm no longer on a pedestal am I? You just in the blink of an eye snatched my ass off that podium. (Mind you she is still laughing) Good. It took me a minute to realize what she had just orchestrated. I then slowly started to laugh with her. My only response was, "You fucking genius".

I loved that she orchestrated this because it is extremely hard to be comfortable and be yourself around someone who is in awe of you or someone you are in awe of. From that day forward, I felt Octavia began to relax and be herself or should I say, I was able to relax and be myself around her. It made a world of difference to our friendship.

So as you can see, I learned so much from Octavia, whether she was teaching verbally or through her written word or her warped sense of humor.

CHAPTER 6

TRANSITION

On occasion, Octavia would complain about the medications her doctor had prescribed. How the medications interfered with her writing and ability to concentrate. How she would be prescribed one medication for an illness and another for the side effects of the first one and another for the side effects of the second one, and so on and so on. Octavia detested having to take them. I didn't know the severity of her illness. She never told me. Because I was in Maryland and she in Washington, I couldn't see.

Monday, February 27, 2006, started out like most Mondays – uneventful. The weekend was a faint memory, and I was back to the daily grind in the office. As usual, I scrolled through R&B singer Lalah Hathaway's website. A friend by the name of Torrance (Tll) had posted what I assumed to be a tribute to Octavia. After all, it was Black History Month, and in celebration, all month Torrance was writing tributes to great African Americans and posting them on Lalah Hathaway's message board. It made perfect sense to me that he was writing a tribute to Octavia. I felt so proud. I skimmed the post, but later returned to read the entry in its entirety. The headline shook me to my core.

Science Fiction Writer Octavia Butler Dies.

The news of Octavia's death devastated me. Tears streamed down my cheeks. I found myself gasping for air. I didn't know who to call or who to turn to. I walked out of my office, got into my car, and drove around the Baltimore-Washington Parkway for hours. I was in a daze. Finally, I drove home and went to bed.

When I woke up several hours later, I logged onto the Internet and frantically searched websites for updated information about the circumstances surrounding her death. I was praying that this was just a bad prank. I kept dialing Octavia's telephone number but would never get an answer. I needed to know what had happened to my friend.

I remembered that Octavia mentioned and read that Octavia was friends with authors Tananarive Due and her husband Steven Barnes on one of the websites. After finding an email address, I sent a message to Mr. Barnes. Within thirty minutes, he responded and put me in touch with Leslie Howle, a dear friend of Octavia's who also lived in Seattle.

On Tuesday morning, I was able to pull myself together enough to send an email to Leslie Howle. In the email I tried to explain who I was and left a telephone number asking if she could call me. I wanted to find out when the services were and what happened. A friend was in town working on the set of the HBO television show, *"The Wire"* as one of its stunt persons. She invited me and another friend to the set. While on the set watching her crash up cars, I received a telephone call from Leslie Howle. Leslie stated that Octavia had spoken of me. She also stated that I could attend the services.

That evening, I searched websites for competitive prices for flights departing from Baltimore to Seattle. The memorial service for Octavia was scheduled for Thursday, March 2nd, and a round-trip ticket cost a whopping $1,100. At that time there was absolutely no way I could afford to pay that amount of money.

My head hurt and the pounding in my temples was so intense that I crawled underneath the covers and cried myself to sleep. I felt helpless and at a complete loss. Those who live in only this three-dimensional physical world of persons, places, and things, and ignore the spiritual cannot understand what happened next. Around midnight, a woman's voice woke me up. She instructed me to get out of bed and go to the computer.

I obeyed. For once, I didn't ask any questions or talked back. There was no why or "I'm tired".

I checked the prices again and found a round-trip ticket to Seattle for about $178.00. With tears in my eyes, I booked the flight. I was so grateful that I cried out to the universe, "Thank you. Thank you. Thank you."

On Wednesday, March 1st, I emailed Leslie Howle to alert her that I would be able to attend. She called me back and assured me that I would have an opportunity to speak at Octavia's memorial service. My body immediately went into shock. That was never my intention. I just wanted to be in the company of people who cared about Octavia as I did.

I had no idea what to say and had twenty-four hours to write a tribute.

I boarded the plane headed for Seattle with a heavy heart the morning of March 2nd. My head was still pounding, and I was fighting back tears. I tried to write my tribute, but the words wouldn't come. I experienced a classic case of writer's block but this time I was on a plane with no sunflower seeds and ginger ale. I threw a sweater over my head and cried myself to sleep during the five-hour flight. In my mind's eye, there was Octavia, standing there smiling at me.

I arrived at Seattle-Tacoma International Airport about 12:30 p.m. and hopped on a Metro Transit bus to the hotel. Unfortunately, I had arrived too early. I couldn't check in until 3:00 p.m. I asked the desk clerk if there was a place nearby where I could get a cup of coffee and some breakfast.

He laughed. "Oh, you must be from out of town. This is Seattle, home of the very first Starbucks," he said. "There are at least three different places to get coffee on every corner of Seattle."

Today, that is funny, but at the time, I was in no mood for laughter.

After I got the directions to a local breakfast restaurant, I walked out of the lobby in search of a cup of coffee, a Feta cheese and spinach omelet, and a few turkey sausage links. As I turned the corner, a blast of cold air – similar to Chicago's cold gusts – hit me. The wind was so strong that it pushed me backwards. I heard Octavia's voice in my ear. It sounded as clear as if she were standing right next to me.

"Jacqueline, so this is what it took to get you to Seattle. I tried so many times to get you out here."

How could anyone understand how I felt when she spoke to me? All I could think to say was, "Octavia, why did you leave me?" Tears welled up in my eyes, and I could not hold them in. I held on to the side of a building and just cried my eyes out. I managed to get myself together and continued my journey.

I found the restaurant with no problem and ordered breakfast. I consumed way too much coffee, which has an opposite effect on me. Instead of waking me up, it makes me drowsy. After I had finished my meal, I walked back to the hotel and checked into my room.

I had about five hours before the memorial service, so I tried to write my speech, again. But, I got sleepy and took a quick nap. I woke up with about two and a half hours left until the start of the service. And I still had not written my tribute.

I returned a telephone call to Lalah Hathaway. I met Lalah in March of 2005, became a member of her online message board, and through texting, emails, lunches, and telephone conversations, we had become friends. The talented vocalist had been extremely supportive of me throughout this tragic ordeal. We talked for about thirty minutes. I must give her credit for really calming me down. She told me to write what was on my heart and assured me that everything would turn out fine. She said that she had no doubt that I could pull this off. After speaking with her, I composed myself and the words easily came to mind.

I managed to get dressed and then hailed a cab to the Science Fiction Museum and Hall of Fame at 5th and Harrison Street, on the outskirts of downtown Seattle. Since I had arrived early, I decided to sit in a restaurant and bide my time. While there, I happened to strike up a conversation with a young woman who entered the restaurant and sat near me.

She told me that she was a reporter for a Seattle Newspaper. I introduced myself and said that I was from Laurel, Maryland. As it turned out, she was born in Baltimore, Maryland. What a blessing. The light-hearted conversation distracted me and helped me to calm down. Although she lived in Seattle, she was a die-hard Baltimore Orioles and Baltimore Ravens fan. We talked sports and all things Baltimore. She asked me why was I in Seattle and I told her that I was there for the memorial service for Octavia Butler. This young woman said she was not familiar with Octavia Butler and her works but was sent as a reporter to cover the story. She asked me did I know her and I said, yes she was a dear friend. We talked some more until it was time for the services to start. I entered the area and was seated. I looked around the place and was so nervous.

Finally, the services got underway.

I was jittery – way beyond nervous – and when sitting while nervous, my right leg will rock ohhhhhh about 125 miles-per-hour. As I watched the tribute to Octavia and listened to the many fond remembrances, I realized how truly blessed and fortunate I had been that Octavia had chosen to spend time with me. My heart ached as I sat in my seat and silently cried, while pictures of my friend flashed across a huge overhead projection screen. I could not bear to look up at the pictures on a screen.

God, I miss her so much, I thought.

I kept zoning in and out and could not to this day tell you who appeared before me and who spoke after me. When it was my turn to speak, I stood. My legs felt shaky, so my focus went into maintaining my balance. I have never really had a fear of speaking in front of a large gathering – it doesn't bother me, oh but this occasion was different. I wasn't sure if I could make it through my speech without becoming too emotional.

As I read my tribute, I noticed that my voice sounded like Alfalfa from The Little Rascals. But after a minute I heard the crowd roar with laughter and it wasn't at me but it was with me. They had relaxed and that caused me to relax. I stood a little taller with a sense of confidence and a strong desire to make Octavia proud of me.

I felt Octavia's presence and I heard her say, "Good job, Jacqueline. I knew you could do it!"

After the completion of my tribute, I returned to my seat. Several people came up after me to pay their tributes to Octavia, as well. Once the service had ended, I found myself surrounded by the crowd. They hugged me; they cried on my shoulders. They grabbed my hands. It scared me for a second, but I understood the need. Then, they began to ask me for my business card. I didn't have any. So, I spent a lot of time that night writing down my email address on scrapes of paper.

As I was busy scribbling down my address, I heard Octavia's voice, once again.

"Jacqueline, you are so hard headed. I told you seven years ago to get those damn cards."

All I could do was shrug my shoulders and chuckle.

Here is an excerpt of the article written in the Seattle Newspaper

Published 1000 pm, Friday, March 3, 2006,

"Although Ellison made the crowd chuckle with

recognition of the Butler they knew -- to him she was

Estelle -- it wasn't until Jacqueline Harris told her story that they allowed themselves to laugh, really laugh in a much-needed cathartic release. She flew in from Laurel, Md., to say goodbye to the friend she met seven years ago over the phone. She had gone online to look up Butler's address to write to her and tell her how much she liked her books.

"A telephone number popped up. I thought it was an agent," Harris told the crowd. "She told me, 'I am not on the Internet.' I told her, 'Would you please give me her address, and I want to write my favorite author.' She said, 'you are talking to Octavia Butler. You have called my home.' I thought life is not that easy. She spent 30 minutes trying to convince me who she was."

Thirty minutes turned into a five-hour conversation. Years later, Butler visited Baltimore for a sci-fi convention and took Harris around the city to places she researched for her well-known "Kindred," a time-travel novel that takes *readers on a journey with a modern-day black woman trapped in pre-Civil War Maryland, a Dixie-leaning state sheathed in Yankee colors.*

"Who knew this phone conversation would bloom into a friendship?" Harris said.

Even those who did not know her personally felt as though they did, so powerfully did her words speak to them."

Once the museum had cleared out, I went for a drive around Seattle with several of the women who had attended the service. After they returned me to the hotel, I went to my room and immediately called Lalah Hathaway to tell her how things had gone at the memorial service. I also thanked her for all of her support. I then showered and attempted to go to sleep, but I couldn't. I sat up in the bed and just cried. All I could think of was the pain and fear I assumed Octavia felt when she fell outside of her home. Plus, the fact that she was alone was a little too much for me to handle. I was feeling the pain and fear that I thought she went through. My heart was grieving and I had gotten to the point where I could no longer cry, which frightened me.

After pacing the hotel floor, I put on some clothes and went out walking around the hotel until I got tired. I returned to my room and finally got into the bed, attempting to go to sleep. I lie there for about five minutes. All of a sudden, I felt pinned down and not able to move. I was not frightened at all, though. My friend Octavia Estelle Butler said the following words that stopped this descending state of grief that I was on.

Octavia stated, "Jacqueline, please pull yourself together. I made my transition before I hit the ground."

Those words allowed me to immediately center myself, and I peacefully went to sleep.

The next day, I toured the city of Seattle. It was a marvelous city to tour. The first Starbucks, the sports stadium, the area where the salmon jumps out of salt water into fresh water or vice verse and so many other sites. I toured the area with an older couple from Japan, a couple from Australia, someone from Boston and three people from Canada. One of my favorite moments and I am sure

Octavia would have gotten a kick out of was the reserved and stoic couple from Japan. They sat across from me on the tour bus and would only nod their heads and smile. That is until we drove by the baseball stadium. They jumped up and demanded that the driver stop the bus. Why? They wanted to take a picture with the statue of Japan's native son Ichiro Suzuki that was outside the baseball stadium. It made me smile and feel all warm inside to see the pride in their eyes as they got off the bus and took pictures.

Later that night I went to dinner with Leslie Howle. We sat in the restaurant looking like two wounded birds. Our hearts ached. She said that Octavia had spoken to her about me. Then, she said it was up to me to continue in her footsteps.

"Jackie, you have to carry the torch and continue her work."

"No freaking way could I ever," I said, with an expression on my face that bordered on contempt. I mean I thought no one could carry her torch. We sat, ate and consoled each other. Leslie was a magnificent and supportive person to so many of us that day. I will always remember this.

CHAPTER 7

CLOSURE

I titled this book, Lessons Learned From My Friendship With Octavia E. Butler, because that is exactly what she personified to me. She was always teaching and always patience and always a friend. Whether it was the thousands of rejection letters she'd receive or the patience in dealing with an impatient person like others, and myself, she endured. I was sure that early on I was quite the annoyance to her with all of the questions I would ask her. But I eventually found that she was the same way. I loved it and loved answering (if I could) her questions. I could also tell that she enjoyed answering my questions because it meant I was taking the time to get to know her. Many people don't want you to treat them like this celebrity on a pedestal. They want you to get to know them. For the ones who took the time to get to know Octavia, I am sure they found it was such a delight.

It's been over ten years since Octavia made her

transition, and I still had a huge hole in my heart. I would have moments of tears but completing this book helped me to realize why. Losing Octavia was not only a huge loss to me but to the world, but she left a body of work that has/will enhance the world for years to come. Octavia did her job and she fulfilled her purpose. She always uses to say, if you didn't know your purpose, then create your own. She touched so many lives and in people grieving publically on social media, to me in person and privately helped me. As I mentioned earlier, because losing Octavia hurt so much, I found myself blocking out the bad memories. Because I did that, I found out that I was also blocking out the good memories, the lessons learned from her, and the similarities in the lives we've shared. Things that would help me move from one point to the next. It was like I became stuck at that point of her transition. Not only stuck but stuck with amnesia. Which was a horrible and painful place to be. Yes I got a lot of people telling me to work through it, get over it, or you act as if you've known her your entire life. I tried but as I said, there was always a spiritual connection between us. I felt as if when Octavia entered the planet from her previous location, I came from the same place. Sometimes I wonder if I followed her here. It was like we were from the same filament. It took a long time to repair this filament but it is done. Now I can stand up straight, move forward with my life and enjoy the friendship, laughter, tears and lessons taught to me by the patient Octavia Estelle Butler. Now I have always been one who knows that in this vast galaxy, we don't just travel around the sun so many times, call them years and that is it for us. I know that I will see Octavia again and I will give my sister the biggest hug ever and tell her how much I appreciate her patience with me. How much I appreciated her works and the determination she stuck too so that she could finish her work. I would tell her how much the world has missed her. I would tell her how I am so much of a better person because of the lessons learned from her…Even though she would feign protest. I am sure that she would smile and would hug me back. Thank you Octavia and thanks to you the reader.

Photo taken by Jonel Daphnis of Melanin Body Photography

The above picture was taken at a Bust Dedication service for Octavia Butler in Vermont. I was so proud to tell the people about Octavia and our friendship.

    Octavia definitely touched and changed so many others and me because she represented change to the world. My job is to touch others and influence change for the better of the world as she did. The below quote is one of my favorites written by her. It is so profound and really puts all that we do in perspective.

"**All That You Touch, You Change, All That You Change Changes You. The Only Lasting Truth Is Change. God Is Change.**"

The End

ABOUT THE AUTHOR

Jacqueline D. Harris is an Author, Speaker, Publisher and Life Coach. This is her third book as she is also the author of the well-loved books, ***Eliminating a Stagnant Lifestyle*** and ***Healing and Freedom Through These Sacred Tone Masters*** also available at www.sacredtonemasters.com and at www.amazon.com.

Jacqueline was born and raised in Chicago, Illinois graduating from Chicago State University. She has always been a writer of stories, and an obsessive lover of traveling, museums, music and reading.

www.ingramcontent.com/pod-product-compliance
Lightning Source LLC
Chambersburg PA
CBHW070938160426
43193CB00011B/1737